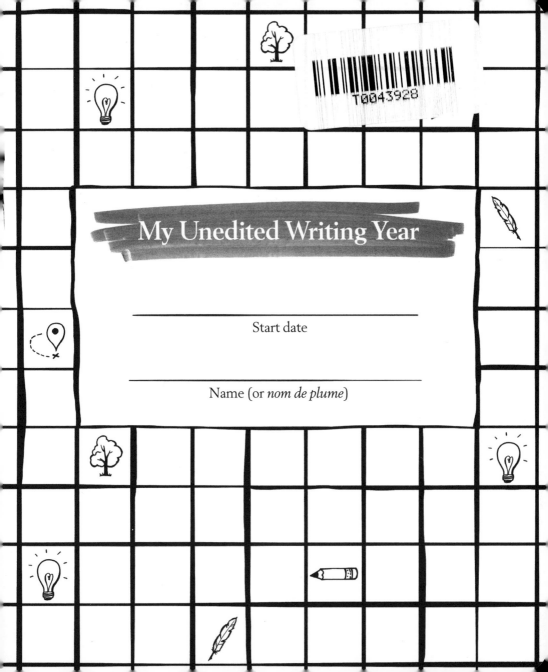

My Unedited Writing Year

_____

Start date

_____

Name (or *nom de plume*)

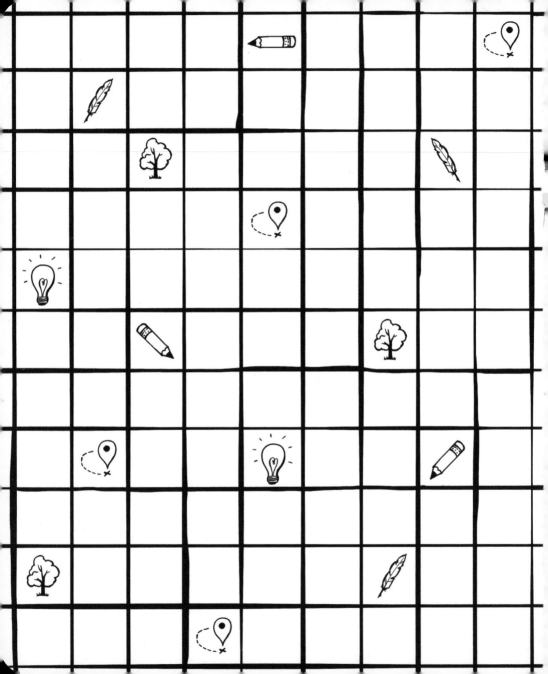

My
Unedited
Writing
Year

Hope Lyda

HARVEST HOUSE PUBLISHERS
EUGENE, OREGON

Dedicated with affection to three generations of women:

Toby Joy, Gina Mammano, and Nora Hope

Acknowledgments:

A heartfelt thanks to Heather Green, who championed this book, and the amazing Harvest House team behind it: Kim, Todd, Peggy, Jeff, Barb, Nicole, Adrienne, and Kari. Special thanks to my sister/text-accessible editor, Dawn Cadwell; my folks; and my support network: Melissa Hart, Cara Strickland, Kimberly Shumate, Carolyn McCready, LaRae Weikert, Shelby Zacharias, Pam Farrel, Jean Jones, Lisa Radosovich, Kim Kidd, Jackie Saling, Dawn Krenz, Nancy Shoptaw, Kari Vorvick, Terry Glaspey, Marc Lyda, Kristen França, my Stillpoint tribe, and so many others. Also, a fond shout-out to Provisions at the Fifth Street Public Market in Eugene, Oregon—my go-to writing space for inspiration and caffeination.

Cover design by Juicebox Design

Interior illustrations and hand lettering by Juicebox Design

My Unedited Writing Year
Copyright © 2019 by Hope Lyda
Published by Harvest House Publishers
Eugene, Oregon 97408
www.harvesthousepublishers.com

ISBN 978-0-7369-7917-7 (pbk.)

Printed in China

19 20 21 22 23 24 25 26 27 / RDS-AR / 10 9 8 7 6 5 4 3 2 1

This Is Your Year

The writer is an explorer. Every step is an advance into a new land.
Ralph Waldo Emerson

Discover the freedom of a welcoming page. Here are 365 invitations to the new landscape of creative sparks, story starts, genius genesis, book inklings, worlds of words, life and faith insights, and "Where did *that* come from?" imagination. Interact with this book from start to finish or follow the icons to write topic by topic:

Writing Practice & Nonfiction

Life Journey

Spiritual Inspiration

Fiction & Poetry

Creativity Jump Starts

May this be a life-changing year for you, dear doodler, journaler, list maker, poet, memoirist, blogger, daydreamer, word collector, corporate creative, author, brainstormer, life coach, spiritual director, writing group leader, lucky person with a favorite pen.

You are an explorer.

Writing Opportunities

1	24	47	70	93	116	139	162
2	25	48	71	94	117	140	163
3	26	49	72	95	118	141	164
4	27	50	73	96	119	142	165
5	28	51	74	97	120	143	166
6	29	52	75	98	121	144	167
7	30	53	76	99	122	145	168
8	31	54	77	100	123	146	169
9	32	55	78	101	124	147	170
10	33	56	79	102	125	148	171
11	34	57	80	103	126	149	172
12	35	58	81	104	127	150	173
13	36	59	82	105	128	151	174
14	37	60	83	106	129	152	175
15	38	61	84	107	130	153	176
16	39	62	85	108	131	154	177
17	40	63	86	109	132	155	178
18	41	64	87	110	133	156	179
19	42	65	88	111	134	157	180
20	43	66	89	112	135	158	181
21	44	67	90	113	136	159	182
22	45	68	91	114	137	160	183
23	46	69	92	115	138	161	184

185	208	231	254	277	300	322	344
186	209	232	255	278	301	323	345
187	210	233	256	279	302	324	346
188	211	234	257	280	303	325	347
189	212	235	258	281	304	326	348
190	213	236	259	282	305	327	349
191	214	237	260	283	306	328	350
192	215	238	261	284	307	329	351
193	216	239	262	285	308	330	352
194	217	240	263	286	309	331	353
195	218	241	264	287	310	332	354
196	219	242	265	288	311	333	355
197	220	243	266	289	312	334	356
198	221	244	267	290	313	335	357
199	222	245	268	291	314	336	358
200	223	246	269	292	315	337	359
201	224	247	270	293	316	338	360
202	225	248	271	294	317	339	361
203	226	249	272	295	318	340	362
204	227	250	273	296	319	341	363
205	228	251	274	297	320	342	364
206	229	252	275	298	321	343	365
207	230	253	276	299			

1

 We spend so much time on our devices. Get used to writing on the expanse of a page by trying out a few pens. Which one is the right fit for your unedited writing year? Write a one-line intention or prayer for the year with each pen.

Idea: While you're shopping for pens, choose a notebook for the overflow of inspiration and ideas this 365-day journey will offer.

2

 Wordsmith Shakespeare penned the famous: "To be, or not to be, that is the question." The better question is: What personal, original phrase or quip of yours might catch on?

Ding-Dong. Special Delivery! A miniature poodle is sitting on your porch. On her forehead is a sticky note which reads: "Read me, then feed me." A scroll is clipped to her jeweled collar. What does it say, and what happens next?

Start your day by writing.

Write a permission slip for yourself to do something, to be something, or to create something you've held back from pursuing.

PERMISSION SLIP

I, _____ , HEREBY GIVE MYSELF PERMISSION TO DO THE FOLLOWING:

_____

_____

_____

_____

SIGNED, X _____

✎ **A Book in You #1.** You have a book in you. This series of prompts scattered throughout will walk you through the book creation process. Do you have an idea? Write a brief description of the book you want to write and choose a genre: memoir, fiction, advice, devotional, tell-all, scholarly contribution, etc.

6

Word of the Day. When you see these Word-of-the-Day prompts with words or phrases to get the mind rolling and the writing flowing, go in any direction. No rules, just writing. Your first prompt is: *Clean slate.*

Write two prayers using the haiku poem structure—which is three lines with five, seven, and five syllables, respectively. A true haiku is about nature, but you can direct yours however you'd like.

Example:

Creation reveals
Your love so wild and honest
My sorrow grows wings

8

You are a botanist. A plant peep. You have just encountered a specimen that nobody has ever noted in journals. This plant is the most amazing creation you've ever seen. Describe it. Draw it, even. How does it make you feel? Are you tempted not to share it?

Money is no object! Create your bucket list right here, right now.

1.

2.

3.

4.

5.

6.

7.

8.

9.

10.

Body Prayer #1. When you see these prompts, write a prayer or meditation for the given focal area of your body along with insights about how your body has served your life.

Start with the *head/mind/brain:* Express thanksgiving, perhaps for knowledge, problem solving, and a mind that creates. Release spiral thoughts.

11

Uh-oh. Pets can pen memoirs. Who knew? Write a first-person (is "first-cat" a thing?) account of what your pet or someone else's pet has written in its first chapter.

In your honor, a library is curating a special collection of books to go in a fancy new wing. Which genres and books will make the cut? Do you have any unique requests for the design of the room?

Turn your attention to a secondhand object. Write about its journey or about an imagined previous owner.

List six ways you plan to commit to, preserve, and indulge in the joy of writing and creating. (You are holding one of them.)

1.

2.

3.

4.

5.

6.

"Writing, the creative effort, the use of the imagination, should come first—at least for some part of every day of your life. It is a wonderful blessing if you will use it. You will become happier, more enlightened, alive, impassioned, lighthearted and generous to everybody else."[1]

Brenda Ueland

15

🌳 **Silent Retreat #1.** A few retreat prompts will help you settle into the richness of silence. Get in a comfortable seated position and be still for five minutes. If you'd like, start the time by thinking, *Be present to God and Mystery.* When you're done, write the thoughts, discomforts, or ideas that came to mind.

"The job of the artist is always to deepen the mystery."
Frances Bacon

16

Open a dictionary, book, or web page and choose five random words. Write those here and make up a definition for each.

17

You've been asked to be a guest host on a late-night talk show. Who are your musical, celebrity, or people-of-interest guests? What happens?

_____

_____

_____

_____

_____

_____

_____

_____

_____

_____

_____

_____

_____

_____

_____

_____

_____

_____

Turn your page sideways to see if that expands your writing mind.

Scribe a letter to your younger self at whichever age you choose. Give advice, warnings, wisdom, or encouragement that your younger self was longing for at the time.

19

Describe your version of the ultimate writing room, nook, or studio. Could this be realized in your current home? Jot down a plan to incorporate some of your ideas into an area where you write.

Create a "God is" list. Start each sentence with "God is…" and finish with a characteristic, a metaphor, a proclamation. Whatever comes to mind. Try for a list of at least 15 items so you stretch beyond first thoughts.

21

💡 Build the travel itinerary for your dream trip.

22

Fill the box with nouns. Put a mark by those that spark the impulse to start writing a personal story, novel, poem, riddle, fable, etc. Now write to fill the rest of the page.

23

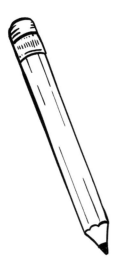

Write a brief announcement describing your morning as if it were breaking news.

24

Write one of your established family stories…except give it a fantastical, fictional twist.

25

💡 Word of the Day: *lightning bugs*

 Describe a place you've been just once: a faraway location, a town where you gassed up your car, a newly discovered hiking trail. Tap into all the senses for the description. Imagine all layers: sky, ground, horizon, backdrop, tangibles, thoughts, mood.

27

💡 If I've said it once, I've said it a million times…

Describe your pilgrim road. What would you call the place where you stand today?

_____

_____

_____

_____

_____

_____

_____

_____

_____

_____

_____

_____

_____

_____

_____

_____

_____

"Take a look at the pilgrim road and see where you have come from and where you are going."[2]

Eugene Peterson

29

Get your pen ready. Now scribe "I am a writer" 15 times. Describe how you feel after that exercise.

Congrats! You've made this writing practice a habit.

Make up a recipe. Think through the ingredients, instructions, and serving suggestions. Let your mind work through the process of creating.

_____

_____

_____

_____

_____

_____

_____

_____

_____

_____

_____

_____

_____

_____

_____

_____

_____

_____

_____

_____

_____

_____

31

Postcard to Self. Write a note to yourself as if from a submarine.

Here is a writing prompt from author Susan Zimmermann that might help you identify a place of stuckness: "Write about the one thing that is hardest for you to deal with. Begin with 'I have come a long way. But I can't stop thinking about…'"[3]

Write a blessing for someone you barely know. Think of others to write blessings and wishes for and keep the love flowing.

Example:

May _____ feel the gift of mercy for this season of life.

Writing Sprint. Use sprints to break open the thoughts and clear cobwebs. No second-guessing. Go for it. Choose one of these words to be your jumping-off point for a ten-minute writing session: *reckless, canyon, delight, spaghetti.*

Try writing your first sentence with your nondominant hand.

Outside the bowl, right down a few of your needs. Inside the bowl, write what could be placed in such a vessel to sate those needs right now. Use words, phrases, prayers, descriptions, whatever! Consider this a serving of the ultimate comfort food…nourishing food for thought.

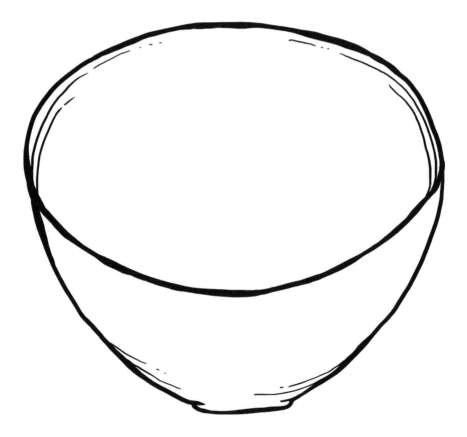

Poet Langston Hughes claimed, "My best poems were all written when I felt the worst. When I was happy, I didn't write anything."[4] Write a fictional scene of a writer having a very bad personal day which, in turn, fosters a winning writing day.

37

 Write about a moment in your childhood, emphasizing the smells.

38

Actively collect and invent words this week. Gather them here. Start today with a list of several fralishous made-up words!

"The great thing about collecting words is they're free; you can borrow them, trade them in or toss them out...Words are lightweight, unbreakable, portable, and they're everywhere. You can even make them up. Frebrent, bezoncular, zurber."[5]

Susan G. Wooldridge

A trapeze artist and a physicist are on a cross-country road trip. You're one of them. Which? What was the catalyst for this adventure?

_____

_____

_____

_____

_____

_____

_____

_____

_____

_____

_____

_____

_____

_____

_____

_____

_____

_____

_____

_____

_____

Write an acrostic poem or prayer using the letters of one of these words: *grace, renew, prayer, hope, mercy,* or a word you choose.

Example:

G oodness flows strong and steady
R ounding up debris,
A ltering my inner path of resistance,
C arving new outlets, forming
E ver-widening channels of hope

What's the biggest compliment you ever received? How did it impact you?

Try writing with a different color of ink.

42

Set a writing date with a friend. Decide where to meet, when, and for how long. Use this space to make your plans or return to it afterward and describe how it felt to write with someone. Did your energy change? Did you find yourself wondering what they were writing? Will you do it again?

 Create a word trail on a topic. Start with one word and then, without adding a space, write another word which begins with the last letter of the initial word. And so on. Keep going for whatever time you allot. Let this be a free-flow exercise related to any topic.

Brief example: *birdssoarrobinnesttreeeagleegrettalon...*

44

You thought you entered a drawing to win a Saturn car, but it turns out you won the chance to be the first earthling sent to communicate with beings discovered on one of Saturn's moons! Prepare your message.

45

✎ **A Book in You #2.** Without overthinking it, respond to these two questions about your book: Why should this book exist in the world? Why are you the one to write it?

Describe the view from a hot-air balloon. What are you soaring above? What do you see? How does this experience change more than your view?

List six ways you were creative as a youth. Are any of these ways you express creativity today? Have any of these become a part of your occupation? Is there one you would like to reintroduce to your world? Reflect on the list and write about anything that comes to mind.

48

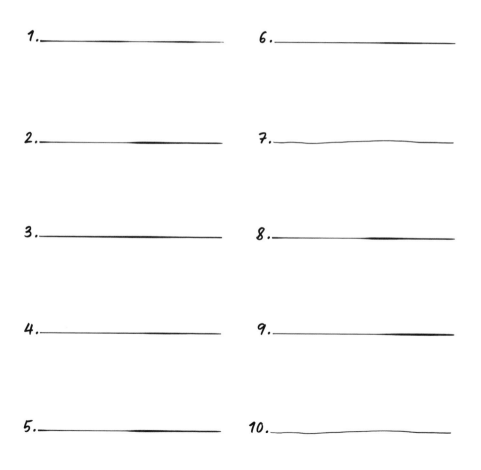

Create ten "ghost names"—pseudonyms—for yourself. (Louisa May Alcott used Aunt Weedy, Flora Fairfield, and Minerva Moody, among others.) Which would you use for the various roles in your life (real or imagined)?

1._____   6._____

2._____   7._____

3._____   8._____

4._____   9._____

5._____   10._____

 **Body Prayer #2.** *Shoulders:* Recall how you have carried many things on your literal and figurative shoulders. Write about your appreciation for those times of extra strength and perseverance. What weight do you need to remove from your shoulders and place in God's hands?

50

Time for some writing roulette. Grab a favorite book, pick a random page, and use the first or last full sentence on the page to start writing your own creation here.

Return to something you've written and underline anything that surprises you.

51

Write out your full name. See how many words you can create using the various letters.

_____

_____   _____

_____   _____

_____   _____

_____   _____

_____   _____

_____   _____

_____   _____

_____   _____

_____   _____

_____   _____

_____   _____

Write an "I am" list. Start each sentence with "I am…" and finish with anything and everything. Try for at least 15 "I am" phrases. The longer the list, the sillier and deeper you can get.

I am

I am

I am

I am

I am

I am

I am

I am

I am

I am

I am

I am

I am

I am

I am

53

✎ Do a ten-minute writing session about the night sky.

_____

_____

_____

_____

_____

_____

_____

_____

_____

_____

_____

_____

_____

_____

_____

_____

_____

_____

_____

Share the birth story of one of your writings, your artistic creations, or your personal sense of calling. What are you currently being called to cocreate?

_____

_____

_____

_____

_____

_____

_____

_____

_____

_____

_____

_____

_____

_____

"All of us who have given birth to a baby, to a story, know that it is ultimately mystery, closely knit to God's own creative activities which did not stop at the beginning of the universe. God is constantly creating, in us, through us, with us, and to co-create with God is our human calling."[6]

Madeleine L'Engle

Describe the hands of a loved one.

Put on a hat, fake mustache, wig, or some outfit you create and write as this impromptu character. Need a topic? Write about this character's view of karaoke or tiny dogs.

Idea: If you are in the process of writing a novel, dress as one of those characters and work on your story for an hour.

57

💡 Word of the Day: *Chinese food*

💡 **Postcard to Self.** Write a note to your current self from a time when you felt more inspired. It's a time-travel pep talk.

Dear Me,

To: Me

Craft four brief messages of encouragement to your spirit. Each message needs to be six words or fewer.

1.

2.

3.

4.

Make a list of three places you have lived. Respond to any or all of these prompts for each one:

1. What is the first thought that comes to mind when you recall this residence?

2. Which aspects of this place brought you joy or annoyed you?

3. Describe sounds, people, meals, music, worries, or hobbies that were a part of your life here.

 **Writing Sprint.** Choose a word to be your jumping-off point for a ten-minute writing session: *lemons, barriers, shrill, hot-air balloon.*

When you write, do you surround yourself with various writing voices and genres or lean into silence and inner cues? Why?

_____

_____

_____

_____

_____

_____

_____

_____

_____

_____

_____

_____

_____

_____

_____

_____

_____

"Some writers are the kind of solo violinists who need complete silence to tune their instruments. Others want to hear every member of the orchestra—they'll take a cue from a clarinet, from an oboe, even."[7]

Zadie Smith

List seven power words for your life. Write about the one that is most empowering for you right now.

64

Write a prayer of thanksgiving for something you used to view as a burden.

Adopt a new word every day and work it into your writing exercise.

Turn a classic story into a contemporary movie. What story do you choose, and how do you make it contemporary? (The classic can be a children's book, a novel, a fable, etc.)

_____

_____

_____

_____

_____

_____

_____

_____

_____

_____

_____

_____

_____

_____

_____

_____

_____

_____

 Mirror, mirror. Look at your reflection in a mirror for five minutes. As observer instead of owner, look at each eye, your lips, your ears, your face's shape, your laugh lines. After that time, write a description in this face about what you saw in *that* face. Vulnerability? Strength? Worry? Openness?

What's your style? Describe it, shape it, claim it here.

68

 Do a ten-minute writing session on whatever is occupying your mind today.

As a nonfiction exercise, rewrite Dickens's famous novel opening for *A Tale of Two Cities* to create your own descriptive commentary of *these* times.

"It was the best of times, it was the worst of times, it was the age of wisdom, it was the age of foolishness, it was the epoch of belief, it was the epoch of incredulity, it was the season of light, it was the season of darkness, it was the spring of hope, it was the winter of despair."

Charles Dickens

Body Prayer #3. *Eyes, ears, mouth:* How have these features allowed you to connect with others, speak up for yourself or your family, sing praises, express emotions, pay attention to your life, notice beauty? When have they been closed? When do you wish they had been closed? Reflect and then write a prayer about what these thoughts bring up.

Describe the ocean in detail without using the words *blue* or *wave*.

Draw three picture frames below. In the frames write words that describe 1) how you think others see you, 2) how you picture yourself, and 3) how you want to be seen.

Writing Sprint. Choose a word to be your jumping-off point for a ten-minute writing session: *rooster, catawampus, storm cloud, liver and onions.*

Create a schedule for the perfect writing day. Now describe what your real one looks like.

_____

_____

_____

_____

_____

_____

_____

_____

_____

_____

_____

_____

_____

_____

_____

_____

_____

_____

75

A spiritual leader experiencing a yearlong crisis of faith witnesses a waitress get fired for giving an extra meal to a family in need. Write what happens next in this story.

76

Reflect on your first day of kindergarten, middle school, high school, or college. Write about it in either first person or third person.

First-person example:

I walked into the cavernous, humid gym, anxiously looking for a familiar face.

Third-person example:

Hope held her notebook close to her chest. From beneath the protective screen of her too-long bangs, her eyes scanned the room in search of someone in charge.

 I remember when…

Become a better listener and you'll become a better writer.

Go on a progressive poem-writing journey. In your first location, write a few lines. Draw inspiration from the setting. At your second and then third locations, keep expanding your poem. In the margin, list the locations to remember your journey. This is your unedited writing year, so no fancy poetry rules required. You can even write a poem with only one to two words per line in fifteen lines. Freedom!

79

Postcard to Self. Write a note to yourself as if from an urban penthouse roof deck.

Spiritual Will #1. You can write a spiritual will at any age. This is a personal document that expresses who you are and presents the hopes, thoughts, and prayers you want to leave for others. There will be a few prompts throughout the book; here is the first: *The beliefs that matter most to me are...*

A Book in You #3. Who do you imagine will be your reader? Craft a detailed character description of this reader so you can think of him or her while you write your book. What's their name, occupation, favorite hobby? Dig in to wildly specific details for this reader profile.

Create a *Jeopardy!* game show topic based on your life. Remember that this show states an answer, and the question is the missing piece. Write seven answers and then, next to each, write the winning question. If you have a writing group, consider playing a round or two together.

Example:

A: Blue, hairless bunny. Q: What was my favorite stuffed animal as a child?

83

Your life is the answer to what question?

84

Write about a time you experienced God as a sound. As a color?

🌳 Pray in a new way today. Draw, color, walk, write a poem, dance, sing, hike, or contemplate a view or element of nature. Write about how this form of prayer felt. Any surprises?

With the quote below from amazing food writer M.F.K. Fisher as inspiration, write about a recent meal.

"It seems to me that our three basic needs, for food and security and love, are so mixed and mingled and entwined that we cannot straightly think of one without the others. So it happens that when I write of hunger, I am really writing about love and the hunger for it."[8]

M.F.K. Fisher

87

An interview goes insanely, comically wrong. Write as a short story or a scene of dialogue.

_____

_____

_____

_____

_____

_____

_____

_____

_____

_____

_____

_____

_____

_____

_____

_____

_____

_____

_____

_____

88

Word of the Day: *Tree house*

Map your life so far. Draw a meandering path through this page to represent your journey. Depict different life events and moments with symbolic elements. For example, use bridges (for a move or change), cliffs (for risks), highways, rocky paths, deserts (for spiritual or physical struggles), etc.

Scribe a love letter to someone. An unrequited love interest in middle school. Your spouse. Your beloved dog.

You are bringing God to an elementary school show-and-tell class. What do you show? What do you tell?

92

⊙ What recent idea did you deem a bad one that could actually be a good
one?

Create a comic strip inspired by a funny moment in your life.

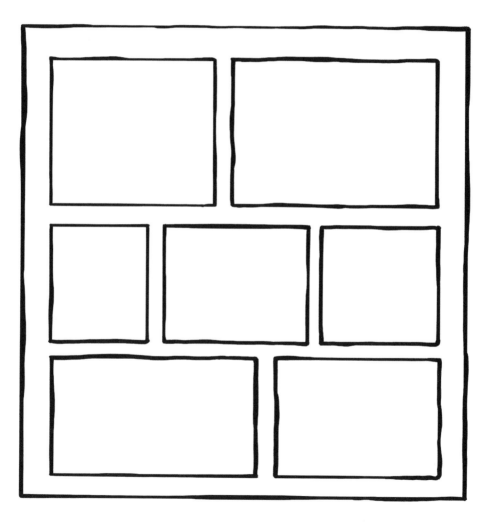

✏ Go ahead, confess something.

You'll probably think I'm crazy, but...

List 10 things going right in your life right now. You can do it.

_____

_____

_____

_____

_____

_____

_____

_____

_____

_____

_____

_____

_____

_____

_____

_____

_____

_____

_____

_____

Imagine you find a message in a bottle. What does it say? How does it impact you?

Postcard to Self. Write a note to your current self from a time when you felt homesick.

Dear Me,

To: Me

 Let's do a reverse Mad Libs experiment. Write a short scene or story incorporating these words in any order:

Nouns: *robot, meatball sandwich*

Verbs: *escape, invent*

Adverbs: *hastily, tediously*

Adjective: *mysterious*

Describe a time you've had a "mountaintop" experience—an encounter with God in a memorable, powerful way.

100

Describe your imaginary friend. (If it is ready to be seen, you can draw it too.)

What decision is on your mental plate? Label the options A and B. Now write a fictional paragraph per choice as though you had followed that path and are on the other side of it. You're sampling how each feels. Does anything stand out that helps you make the actual decision?

Option A: _____

Option B: _____

102

Quick! Write 15 random words. Craft a short story or fictional scene including the words you listed.

 You decide to write under a pen name (maybe one you listed for prompt 48?). Which name do you use, and what is the project? How might you feel differently when creating as this persona?

Create a blackout poem! It's simple. Blot out the words you *don't* want and preserve the words you *do* want. Savor this piece by John O'Donohue. Then create your own treasure.

There is a very important distinction to be made between listening and hearing...Sometimes the most important thresholds of mystery are places of silence. To be genuinely spiritual is to have great respect for the possibilities and presence of silence...Poets are people who become utterly dedicated to the threshold where silence and language meet. One of the crucial tasks of the poet's vocation is to find his or her own voice. When you begin to write, you feel you are writing fine poetry; then you read other poets only to find that they have already written similar poems. You realize that you were unconsciously imitating them. It takes a long time to sift through the more superficial voices of your own gift in order to enter into the deep signature and tonality of your Otherness. When you speak from that deep, inner voice, you are really speaking from the unique tabernacle of your own presence. There is a voice within you that no one, not even you, has ever heard. Give yourself the opportunity of silence and begin to develop your listening in order to hear, deep within yourself, the music of your own spirit.[9]

You're a comedian. Yes, you are. Write the first three jokes of your act.

In relation to a current situation, ask God, "What do you want me to notice right now?" Spend time in silence. Write about anything you feel called to pay attention to. Sometimes just by asking the question, a shift takes place.

Create a detective character to be the protagonist in a new mystery series. Describe him or her in great detail, including their physical description, what they like to eat for breakfast, their quirky habits, or what tools of the trade they keep on them at all times.

✎ Write about or list what enslaves you or limits your ability to be creative. Consider habits, negative people, ideas, distractions, past mistakes or attempts, other people's expectations.

"The artist cannot be free in his art if he does not have a conscience that warns him when he is acting like a slave in his everyday life."[10]

Thomas Merton

A Book in You #4. Create an outline for your book. For a starter structure, break the story progression or nonfiction message into three parts, and then break each of those parts down into three to five points in a story line or four to five chapters for a nonfiction message. Change to suit your creation. Summarize each section with one sentence. Go.

If these walls could speak...Oh my. What would they say to you? Would they share stories you have forgotten? Would they remind you of people who have come and gone? Write from the perspective of the walls of your home.

Think of an area of life for which you could use a pep talk. Write one to yourself.

Bring it! The word "prompt" comes from a Latin term meaning "to bring forth."

112

Go sit at a local public place and describe the scene. What is the feel of the environment? What are the moods of the people there, the sights, sounds? Dig into descriptive words and present a word picture of this setting.

Body Prayer #4. *Arms:* What have you gathered in your arms that are a joy and blessing? Children, loved ones, dear pets, a bounty of fresh fruit from an orchard's harvest? List more ways your arms have brought things closer. What about times they helped you keep something at a distance? Write a prayer about all such aspects of the human life.

114

Word of the Day: *Hullabaloo*

Go to a book, magazine, website, or anything with words. Choose five random words from there. Now use each word respectively in the following ways:

1._____

Knock-knock joke:_____

_____

_____

2._____

Command:_____

_____

_____

3._____

Apology:_____

_____

_____

4._____

First sentence in a mystery:_____

_____

_____

5._____

Banner ad for a tire store:_____

_____

_____

Write an obituary for a part of your life you've changed or moved on from, or for a habit you have let go of along the way.

Write your artist manifesto. List what creativity means to you, your intentions for creativity in your life, and what your personal call to create looks like. (Or doodle a self-portrait while you think about your manifesto.)

MY MANIFESTO

(SIGNED)

Write a letter to God. How do you address the divine? How do you sign the letter? What comes up as you engage on the page?

Do a meditation walk for six minutes at a pace that initially feels uncomfortably slow. What arises? Do soul needs make themselves known?

Approach today with curiosity. Don't settle for skimming the surface as you have conversations and encounter information. Use a reporter's toolbox of questions in each situation: Who? What? Why? Where? When? How? Record how this changes your day, your energy, your engagement with others, and your circumstances.

🖋 **Ding-Dong. Special Delivery!** A young girl with purple velvet ribbons in her hair and friendship bracelets stacked on her wrists smiles as you open the door. Before you can call Child Protective Services, she slides a backpack from her shoulders and hands it to you, saying, "Fill this with supplies that delight you." Make your list.

Write about your childhood happy place. What are the sights, sounds, smells, and memories that come to life when you recall this location?

Make a list of adjectives. Then use any of the words to write a story starter or poem.

124

Work on a puzzle as a form of meditation for 15 minutes. What ideas float through your mind as your brain works on piecing together an image? Jot down those thoughts, then write about one of them.

Create a word collage on this page. Write with different pens, styles, and sizes of words and letters. Write from different angles. Have the visual presentation of a word reflect its meaning.

Read aloud something you have written. Do this weekly!

Describe your life right now from the perspective of standing on holy ground.

Spend time listening to your life. What does it say? List some truths from your life experience that you sense will support, fuel, inform, and infuse your current and future writing.

"Listen to your life. See it for the fathomless mystery it is. In the boredom and pain of it, no less than in the excitement and gladness: touch, taste, smell your way to the holy and hidden heart of it...What I started trying to do as a writer and as a preacher was more and more to draw on my own experience not just as a source of plot, character, illustration, but as a source of truth."[11]

Frederick Buechner

Within the square, write words depicting the beliefs, people, problems, or worries that keep you living or thinking inside the box. On the rest of the page, jot down words, goals, dreams, or beliefs that inspire you to dwell outside the box.

Describe your favorite piece of furniture in detail. Give it lots of time and attention. Use descriptive words that stretch your vocabulary.

Spiritual Will #2. *The most meaningful moments of my life so far have been...*

You have an item that will be up for bid in the Sotheby's auction next month. Write a compelling description of the object that is sure to garner a top sale.

Weather can be an evocative scene setter. Describe a weather experience (real or imagined) that scares, moves, or excites you. Use all your senses.

133

💡 **Writing Sprint.** Choose a word to be your jumping-off point for a ten-minute writing session: *angst, juggle, patisserie, outsider.*

Talk with someone who has a different view.

Record details of a dream. Don't worry if it sounds like how a Picasso painting looks. Were people from your life represented? What images or feelings were strongest? Does anything from the dream resonate with your waking life?

A **Book in You #5.** What is the title of your book? Make a list of five possible titles (and subtitles if needed).

You've set aside a Saturday to clean your attic. After moving a box of old games, you notice a thick photo album with a yellowed image of your great-grandmother on the front. You open the large volume, expecting to see photos of your family. Instead, you find…

💡 Did you ever play the game "I'm going on a trip and I'm taking…" during which your group compiled an alphabetical list of items: apple, book, camera, etc.? Create your own alpha-order packing list. Where are you going? Well, a desert island, of course! Pack cleverly.

A _____

B _____

C _____

D _____

E _____

F _____

G _____

H _____

I _____

J _____

K _____

L _____

M _____

N _____

O _____

P _____

Q _____

R _____

S _____

T _____

U _____

V _____

W _____

X _____

Y _____

Z _____

 **Body Prayer #5.** *Hands:* What have your hands held? A new life? A pen, a fishing pole, your mother's apron string? When have they been lifted in a gesture of surrender or hope? When have they reached out to another? Write about these experiences and add a prayer of gratitude over your hands.

Create a word mountain. What phrases form the foundation? Work your way to the top. What word is placed at the apex? When done, think about the significance of this formation for your life right now.

Map your life still to come in the near or far-off future. Invent and explore in timeline form, an actual map design, or free-flow writing.

Notice which words you use most frequently throughout the day.

Choose a painting or piece of art and write a story based on the image depicted.

Idea: Look up classic paintings such as Chagall's *Paris Through the Window* or Van Gogh's *Café Terrace at Night* or Henry Ossawa Tanner's *The Banjo Lesson*.

142

☼ Embark on a writing session about your relationship with play. Don't filter, edit, or judge.

Inspiration: What or who invites you to be playful? Do you resist or jump in?
What did play mean to you as a child?

_____

_____

_____

_____

_____

_____

_____

_____

_____

_____

_____

_____

_____

_____

_____

_____

_____

Yum. Describe a confectionary masterpiece. Does it swirl, twist, drip, crunch, melt? What sugary details capture your attention and appetite? Now describe the sensation of enjoying an indulgent bite of this morsel. Do this from memory or head for a bakery…you decide.

Write your wrong. You get a do-over. A huge one. A small one. You choose. Write the new version of a day, moment, or encounter you are happy to re-create on the page.

Paint a still-life picture with words. Choose a photo, image, tablescape, or scene in your home or office and word-paint the vignette. Think shadows, texture, dimension, layers, shapes, etc.

Ding-Dong. Special Delivery! You haven't had your morning coffee yet, so this 6:30 a.m. disruption had better be good! You open the door to find a gentleman in a tuxedo. He reaches into his vest pocket and retrieves an aged map and a key. He hands you both, smiles, and says, "You have a mystery room in your home. Surprise! You'll need this map, this key, and clothes more durable than those…um…pajamas. Your watch, phone, and sense of direction won't work in there. Ta-ta." Off he goes. And off you go. Write about the adventure.

Postcard to Self. Write a note to yourself as if from the hayloft of a barn on a summer night.

Describe how writing changes the way you see. Write about something you've noticed lately from a new angle or perspective.

"Being an artist alters the way I see. It changes not merely how I view the work of other artists but also how I view the world."[12]

Jan Richardson

149

Go to a home store or look online and gather 12 different paint color names. Write a poem or very short scene that includes those dozen words or phrases.

150

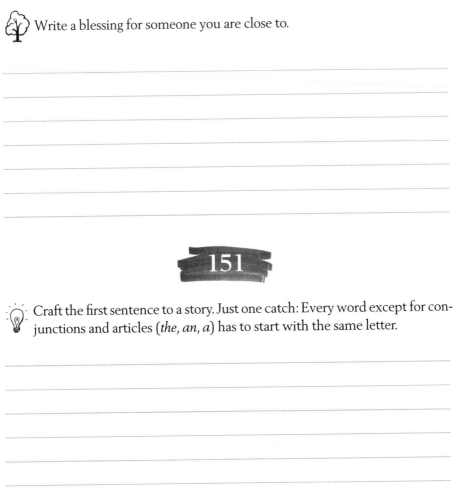

Write a blessing for someone you are close to.

151

Craft the first sentence to a story. Just one catch: Every word except for conjunctions and articles (*the, an, a*) has to start with the same letter.

A couple is having a rather public argument about their financial issues at a bank. They are interrupted by screams coming from the lobby. A robbery is in process, and they are in the office nearest the safe. What happens next?

153

💡 Word of the Day: *Rebellion*

Walk into a room in your home. Stand there for two minutes and then head to another area where that room is not visible. Describe all you saw. Objects, oddities, the placement of furniture, details, and impressions. After ten minutes, put your pen down. Now return to the room. Are you surprised by anything you left out or described less than accurately?

Your city planner invites you to create a meditation garden. Describe your plans in detail. Bring out all those juicy adjectives. How does this exercise awaken your understanding of how setting influences mind-set, mood, peace? Feel free to draw a design.

Write about the earliest holiday you can recall. What tastes, aromas, sights, and sounds inform this recollection?

Go to a new restaurant and then write a review of your dining experience here. Consider posting it online.

Learn a new language to expand your life and love for words.

No matter what you pen, it generates creative momentum. In honor of the beloved creator of Narnia, dear Mr. Lewis, craft a starter scene for a children's fantasy or a scene that would unfold midstory. Anything goes!

"I feel that every time I write a page either of prose or verse, with real effort, even if it's thrown into the fire next minute, I am so much further on."[13]

C.S. Lewis

✐ Draft some plans for a writers' block party. What conversation starters, treats, or activities could turn a block party into a brainstorm?

"I am not at all in a humour for writing; I must write on till I am."

Jane Austen

160

Write a letter to someone from history. Ask questions or share something about your life with them. Did their life's work or choices somehow impact your reality today? Include it all.

161

Think about how this page becomes space for God and a safe container for exploration. Create here. Experiment here. Write a wildly divine idea.

"The arts help us to make space for an encounter with God while also creating a safe container in which to experiment and explore new possibilities."[14]

Christine Valters Paintner and Betsey Beckman

162

Create two lists with the headings "What to Keep" and "What to Get Rid Of."
This writing prompt can relate to stuff, ideas, priorities, habits, etc.

What to Keep

What to Get Rid Of

Today, write until you discover one new thing about yourself.

Become fascinated with something.

164

You are either heroic or insane. You've agreed to take a group of 50 rambunctious fifth graders on an excursion. Where do you dare take them? What happens? What leads to involving the fire department? And why is a chunk of your hair missing?

Write about a moment in your adult life, emphasizing colors.

"As is a tale, so is life: not how long it is, but how good it is, is what matters."

Seneca

Body Prayer #6. *Heart:* Reflect on the ways your physical heart and spiritual heart have served you and made life possible. When have you had your heart broken or blessed? List the ways of the mysterious heart for which you are thankful. What has been placed on your spiritual heart to pray for specifically?

_____

_____

_____

_____

_____

_____

_____

_____

_____

_____

_____

_____

_____

_____

_____

_____

_____

_____

_____

_____

_____

_____

Write an autobiographical reflection poem consisting of one- to three-word lines. Warning…these can be addicting as a writing exercise!

Challenge: Write one of these each day this week. You'll discover new angles to your life, and you'll crack open a window to fresh writing. Here is a snippet from mine:

Buried yet breathing,

Light-seeking

hopeful skeptic.

Yawning resets

bored, worn bones,

scaffolding for creative,

crazy-making mind.

Caffeine comas

eye of brainstorm.

168

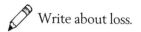 Write about loss.

Practice penmanship as a form of meditation.

169

If these walls could speak…Write from the perspective of the walls in someone else's home, a business, a celebrity or sports hero's estate, a national building, or anywhere that seems like an intriguing place to listen in.

Okay, I have to ask…who is on the short list of actors to play you in the Netflix series based on your life? And what is that series called?

✎ **A Book in You #6.** Work on your first chapter for 30 to 60 minutes. Start here or on your computer; let the words flow. In this space, craft a timeline for writing a rough draft of the book. Consider a chapter per month. These book prompts will address ongoing steps while you keep writing.

How does William Blake's image of God as Poetic Genius expand or change how you think about life, creativity, and love?

"He who loves feels love descend into him and if he has wisdom, may perceive it is from the Poetic Genius, which is the Lord."

William Blake

You're so lucky! The writer you respect most in the world is coming to your area. You get a call that you've been chosen to be their escort for a two-day bookstore tour. But your excitement quickly wanes when you see what they are carrying when you pick them up at the airport. What happens?

Describe a time when you felt larger than life. What led up to the moment? Did the sensation feel like freedom, power, or something else?

175

List as many condiments as you can think of. Try to list them alphabetically. And yes, you can list catsup *and* ketchup, you clever person, you.

176

I reach into my stash of words for today's invitation and emerge with *rest-less, forgive, renewal.* Write a prayer or meditation using all three.

Write about a bittersweet experience. What made it bitter? What made it sweet? Which sentiment describes it best as you recall it in hindsight?

Imagine you are seated at a very large, long table. You can invite anyone from any time or place. Whom do you gather to be with you today?

💡 **Writing Sprint.** Choose a word to be your jumping-off point for a ten-minute writing session: *temptation, parka, cliff-hanger, toupee.*

Silent Retreat #2. Be quiet and still for ten minutes. Let the words *compassion* and *love* be your thoughts as you start the silence. Afterward, write about what arose in your mind and spirit.

What choice, vocation, action, or opportunity scares you so much you suspect it's something you should do? Write as though you have taken the first step in saying yes to this. What does this progress feel like? What has shifted? Is it still scary?

_____

_____

_____

_____

_____

_____

_____

_____

_____

_____

_____

_____

_____

_____

_____

_____

_____

_____

182

You've been told that for the next year you will only have one book to read. What do you choose and why?

183

Write a short reflection about something you do that delights the Creator of the universe. What is one aspect of creation in which you have delighted?

Create seven writing prompts. Consider sharing/swapping with your writing community.

Special assignment: When you are at day 366 and have completed *My Unedited Writing Year,* use your original writing prompts to keep up the habit.

1.

2.

3.

4.

5.

6.

7.

Go to a vintage store and look at postcards or books that have personal notes on them. Write a backstory about the person who wrote or received one of those messages.

List the top three answers you gave as a kid when asked, "What do you want to be when you grow up?" Describe what the allure of each vocation was at the time. Does that aspect still appeal to your adult self? Did those early interests shape your choices?

Our daily word choices become repetitive. List ten ways to say "yes" and ten ways to say "no." Use formal, slang, or invented words. Examples: "Indubitably!" and "Can one-winged bejoppers fly?" Another challenge: Use these in your written or spoken interactions this week.

Yes	No
_____	_____
_____	_____
_____	_____
_____	_____
_____	_____
_____	_____
_____	_____
_____	_____

188

Spiritual Will #3. The characteristics I've admired in colleagues, mentors, friends, and loved ones are characteristics I hope my family and I will always value. They are:

Postcard to Self. Write a note to yourself from the beginning of one of your experiences or journeys.

190

A clown who was hired for a kid's birthday party accidentally shows up at a funeral. What happens?

Your life is a house. Draw the floor plan and label what each room represents. Below the diagram, write a description of what is in each room and how each space feels.

💡 **Writing Sprint.** Choose a word to be your jumping-off point for a ten-minute writing session: *wallow, gasp, fairy tale, waiting room.*

In Julia Cameron's classic book *The Artist's Way*, she encourages writers to go on an artist date with themselves for two hours each week. "Doing your artist date, you are receiving—opening yourself to insight, inspiration, guidance."[15] Use today's page to brainstorm possible outings: Sit at a café featuring live music, walk along the river, wander Home Depot, loiter at a stationery store and try pens. Limitless.

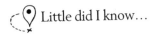 Little did I know…

Describe a vehicle you owned, rented, borrowed, or rode in. Then write about a specific ride. (Maybe it was a crazy rideshare?)

 Congrats! You have won the drawing to name the 12 animals born at the local shelter this season. Better get started; adoptive parents are waiting.

Three kittens

Two puppies

Two iguanas

One llama

One ferret

Two turtles

One chinchilla

 Author Gina Mammano invites us to walk while pondering the words of twelfth-century nun Hildegard of Bingen: I am "a feather on the breath of God." Mammano suggests: "Try to be in tune with your inner landscape as it plays with your outer landscape…What images do the words 'feather' and 'breath' conjure up in your imagination as you reflect on your journey?"[16] Write about this experience.

198

Free day! What's on your mind? Let it all out.

Lately, are you sifting and sorting? Or are you expressing the emergence of change and the need for growth? Explore your answer on the page.

"Writing is a *retrospective* act that helps me sort, sift, and come to terms with my own experience. But it's also a *prospective* act, a Distant Early Warning system about the next opportunity or demand for new growth I need to attend to."[17]

Parker J. Palmer

200

💡 **Writing Sprint.** Choose a word to be your jumping-off point for a ten-minute writing session: *walkabout, chartreuse, mystery, favorite.*

I write in my head all the time. Can you relate? Use your "write brain" today.
First, read this starter sentence: *Against seemingly insurmountable odds, the naive but determined heroine was able to thwart the evil empire with her one surprising skill.* Now go for a mental-writing walk. Return to this page and take dictation from your own clever mind.

Body Prayer #7. *Lungs:* How has your breath powered you and stilled you over the years? What situation has "taken your breath away"?

Consider this breath prayer: Inhale with "I breathe in your goodness, God." Exhale with "I breathe into your presence with peace." Write about all that rises up and all you let go.

203

Describe your happy place as an adult, whether this is a physical place or an emotional one. If you don't have one or you'd like an upgrade, describe the one you want for this season of life.

Tech executives are in desperate need for a new app related to writing. They've asked you to pitch an idea. What is it called? What will it do?

Find a favorite outdoor spot where you can sit and write once a month.

205

💡 Word of the Day: *Wonder*

 **A Book in You #7.** Share your chapters with others who are gentle and honest readers. Take in their feedback and always return to your intention for the message or story before making big changes. In this space, write about anything helpful brought to your attention and make a plan for your rewrites.

**Spiritual Will #4:** I want to share some of the insights I've gathered along my journey:

What I find wonderful about others:

_____

_____

What I find most inspiring about creation:

_____

_____

When I faced loss, this is what I've learned:

_____

_____

Something I wish I had let go of sooner:

_____

_____

A place I treasure is:

_____

_____

A truth I hold on to is:

_____

_____

Describe your family life. Include a detailed look at one family member.

209

Write a brief how-to article or provide a step-by-step guide for a DIY project.

_____

_____

_____

_____

_____

_____

_____

_____

_____

_____

_____

_____

_____

_____

_____

_____

_____

_____

_____

Take time to daydream. Let go of your mental list of tasks and concerns. Sink into your thoughts and see where they lead. Write about what emerges.

Do a crossword puzzle each day.

Craft a 30-second elevator pitch for an invention you think should be in the world marketplace.

 You've been asked to deliver a message this Sunday at a church you've never attended. (They were nice and offered you cookies. You said yes…with your mouth full.) What do you want to share? Write your outline or ideas here.

Ding-Dong. Special Delivery! On your front stoop are three boxes with notes. The first tag reads: "Open with gloves." The second warns: "Open with goggles." And the largest box's note offers: "Open with an open mind." Which do you open and why? What is in the container, and what happens next?

214

How different would your life have been so far if you had a different name? Think of a name. Would you be more or less shy, bold, empowered with that name? Would you have had a different homeroom in school and met different friends? Have fun writing about the possible domino effect.

215

Design a T-shirt. What saying or catchy phrase is on it?

Create a word picture of a house or other dwelling. Use words and phrases expressing what home means to you to form the lines, walls, windows, doors, etc.

You are on the first floor of a lighthouse with three strangers. There is a huge, bulging trash bag in the center of the room. The front door swings open, and a gust of wind rushes in followed by an elderly man riding a miniature pony and carrying a velvet-wrapped box. Tell the story.

218

What baffles you most about God and the world?

Spend time in silence and stillness before you write.

219

Free day! Write what is on your mind or jot down new ideas for stories, poems, changes, etc. that have come to mind during this writing journey so far.

Go to your bookshelf and write down five titles represented. Now craft the first couple paragraphs of a story using all five titles.

You know that mental conversation you've had with someone over and over? Write the script here.

You are a location scout for a movie production company. What is the movie? Oh, I almost forgot—your boss insists you take his surly 15-year-old daughter with you because she is bored. How does your pursuit and final location decision change course because of her?

This quilt is awaiting your personal design. In different sections, add shapes and symbols representing your various life patterns. For example, I would draw circles in one area to represent my pattern of getting stuck in circular thoughts. I might draw equal signs to represent my focus on fairness.

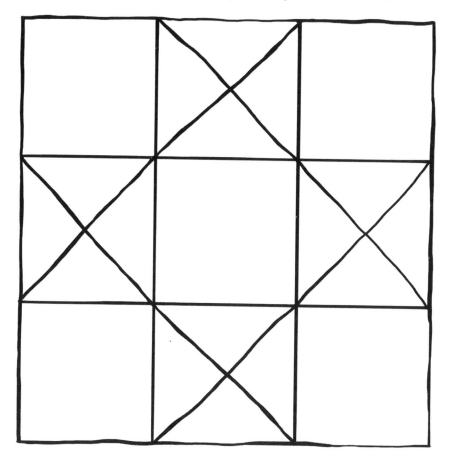

Describe how an animal influenced your life or perspective. This could be a beloved pet or a creature you witnessed in its natural habitat or at a zoo.

225

💡 **Writing Sprint.** Choose a word to be your jumping-off point for a ten-minute writing session: *table, healing, toddler, subway.*

Speak or write a word of hope to someone in need.

Craft a job description. Not just any description! This is to recruit someone to be you for a week. What does it take to be you? What skills (or level
of insanity) does it take?

You are at a very cluttered garage or estate sale. Suddenly you exclaim, "I have always wanted one of these!" What is it? Why is it a find? Are your family and friends surprised to know this about you? Write the tale.

How has spending time in this unedited writing practice shaped your "write direction"? Describe any truths that have been revealed about you, your path, or writing voice. Discuss what kind of writing you are most drawn to and energized by.

Make a list of verbs. Dive into a personal or fictional story inspired by one or all of the verbs.

Time for a close-up. Describe an item that is near you right now. Every edge, ripple, curve, dent. Use words you don't normally associate with the object to expand the mood and dimension of your description. Do you take this item for granted or cherish it? Give drawing it a go.

Silent Retreat #3. Are you ready for a challenge? Choose a comfortable position in which to be still and silent for 15 minutes. Write about the experience. Examine the physical and emotional responses you had to this exercise.

232

What I need to know but keep from myself is...

Make two lists when you go to a bookstore: what to buy and what to write.

Write as an anthropologist studying you. Observe and write *through* this persona to explore your habits, behaviors, traditions, relationships.

💡 **Postcard to Self.** Write a note to your current self from your younger self.

Dear Me,

To: Me

 Word of the Day: *Recess*

Body Prayer #8. *Back:* What have you carried on your back? A younger sibling? A backpack for your college classes or a long hiking trip? When have you stretched out with your back on a warm rock or the soft sand? Jot down memories. Pray your gratitude.

Let's do a mind map. In the center of the page, draw a circle and write "My Thoughts" inside. Draw lines connecting this circle to new ones with words that relate to your thoughts. For example: *worries, hopes, ideas*. Keep going by adding offshoots to these words that get more specific. Let this take you deeper with single-word descriptions, memories, names, emotions.

✎ Are you in waiting mode, or do you have—in hindsight—some apprecia-
tion for a waiting season? Write about the importance of timing in relation
to your calling and craft.

_____

_____

_____

_____

_____

_____

_____

_____

_____

_____

"During the two years when *A Wrinkle in Time* was consistently being
rejected by publisher after publisher, I often went out alone at night and
walked down the dirt road on which Crosswicks faces, and shouted at
God; 'Why don't you let it get accepted? Why are you letting me have all
these rejection slips? You know it's a good book! I wrote it for you! So
why doesn't anybody see it?' But when *Wrinkle* was finally published, it
was exactly the right moment for it, and if it had been published two
years earlier, it might well have dropped into a black pit of oblivion."[18]

Madeleine L'Engle

A Book in You #8. Write your bio for the "About the Author" page in the back of your book.

In this space, create a filled-in crossword puzzle design using words that describe you.

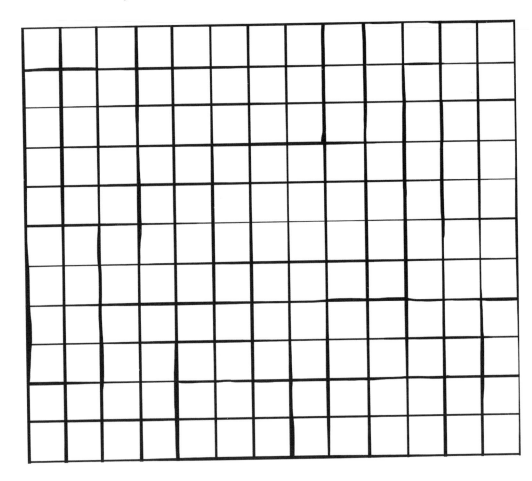

In what area of life are you wanting to be brave? Creativity, provision, purpose? Write yourself through the shift from self-doubt to God-trust, from uncertain to undaunted.

"Bravery is rarely intertwined with a moment of success. It often exists in its purest form in the instant of uncertainty when we turn our feet in a new direction and are trembling with self-doubt."[19]

Hope Lyda

242

You are writing a play based on your life. Write a description of each of the three acts.

243

Look out one of your windows or go to a favorite writing place. Describe the view in detail. Use lots of descriptive words to explain the colors, depth, texture, activity, mood, etc. Sketch any aspect of the setting or an object in view.

244

Surprise! Early this morning, a character from a book you've read or a book you are writing has materialized in your kitchen. Write about the day.

You are a creative director at an ad agency. Your new account is a deodorant that needs a name, along with catchy names for five different scents.

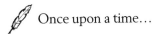 Once upon a time…

Jesus's words were provocative, and his questions often cut to the heart of the matter. Whether the ones below are new to you or familiar, respond as though they are posed directly to you right now. Feel free to focus on one and go deep or do all three. Questions are invitations to know ourselves more fully.

"Do you want to be made well?" (John 5:6 NRSV).

"Why do you look at the speck of sawdust in your brother's eye and pay no attention to the plank in your own eye?" (Matthew 7:3).

"Where is your faith?" (Luke 8:25).

248

Write about a moment in your teen years, emphasizing sound and the sense of hearing.

You are awakened by the sound of your phone's text alert pinging multiple times. You get up, grab the phone, and check your messages. It seems someone has mistakenly contacted your number and is providing the details of where to be to assist with a crime. What do you do? What happens?

250

💡 **Writing Sprint.** Choose a word to be your jumping-off point for a ten-minute writing session: *threshold, dance step, habit, galaxy.*

Write about an image, a theme that will not let you go. Could this be the unforgettable something you should write about for others?

"Your best, your deepest writing, often will not come to you first. You have to follow a kind of trail, allow images to come and go, sketch as visual artists sketch, until you get to...something that holds you (and will hold your reader), something that will not let you go."[20]

Pat Schneider

Spiritual Will #5. I leave to the following people these prayers, hopes, or blessings:

_____ , *from my heart, I give to you:*
(Name)

_____

_____

_____

_____

_____ , *from my heart, I give to you:*
(Name)

_____

_____

_____

_____

_____ , *from my heart, I give to you:*
(Name)

_____

_____

_____

Today, write until you discover one new thing about someone in your life.

Read about a topic you know little of to discover a new "language."

Your plane has to be routed away from your intended destination to an alternate airport. You are hungry and tired and in no mood for a delay. What happens next surprises you and changes your altitude and attitude.

Describe a time when you felt small. Where were you? How did you respond? What words best describe that sense of smallness?

List five of your frequently felt emotions or moods. Under each, write a line of fiction or nonfiction referencing that specific emotion. Here are some emotions to start your brainstorm: *melancholy, elation, fury, sorrow, engagement, loathing, panic, satisfaction.*

1.

2.

3.

4.

5.

Choose one of the emotions you listed in the previous prompt. Now write a nonfiction or fiction scene which illustrates the emotion without naming it.

An elderly man is going to be evicted from his apartment. Only your character can change his fate. Why? How?

_____

_____

_____

_____

_____

_____

_____

_____

_____

_____

_____

_____

_____

_____

_____

_____

_____

_____

_____

_____

_____

Someone just said, "You couldn't write yourself out of a paper bag!" Prove them wrong.

260

In the movie *About a Boy*, the wealthy and unemployed-by-choice main character, Will, divides his day into 30-minute units doing whatever he wants. In this space, list how you would love to use your units from morning till night. Hmm, will writing get any units, or will this be about play and rest?

261

Word of the Day: *Playground*

This is a prayer Flannery O'Connor wrote in the 1940s while she attended the prestigious Iowa Writers' Workshop: "Please don't let me have to scrap the story because it turns out to mean more wrong than right—or any wrong...I don't know, but, dear God, I wish you would take care of making it a sound story because I don't know how, just like I didn't know how to write it but it came."[21]

Write a prayer for divine help with a project. Or journal about a time when you didn't know how to write something, "but it came" nonetheless.

 List ten of your strengths. Which do you depend on most? Which do other people rely on? Have any of these become obstacles? For example, is there a strength you lean on that keeps you from asking for help or taking time for rest and self-care?

Today, use a riddle you've heard or one you find online as a story starter.

Bad day? On the palm of your hand, write a word that makes you laugh.

Think of a time when you made a significant decision. Write as if you had made the other choice. How did that decision impact you and others? How do you feel about the alternate path?

Ding-Dong. Special Delivery! You open the door and are stunned by the glare of bright lights and cameras. You take in the scene of 30 reporters pointing microphones at you. Through the hum of the hubbub you hear, "What is your response to today's events?" What happens next?

You have been asked to speak at a college graduation. What will your message convey? Write a draft here. The scenario is fictional, but let the message be the real deal.

◉ Fill in the blank.

I vote for myself as the most likely person to

_____

Now explain why.

_____

_____

_____

_____

_____

_____

_____

_____

_____

_____

_____

_____

Clean a closet or room to clear writer's block.

You're walking the difficult Camino de Santiago pilgrimage in Spain. On the day you reach the midpoint, the heat is unrelenting, and your right ankle is swollen. You are second-guessing your ability to persevere as you enter a small village and look for a water source. Write about what you experience and whom you encounter on this pivotal day of the journey.

✎ **A Book in You #9.** Write an elevator pitch for your book idea. This is an engaging description of your book's story/message which you can convey in 30 seconds or less. This is helpful in getting others excited about your project!

Fill this page with 40 anythings that inspire gratitude in your life.

 What a coincidence! I...

You are driving to a sci-fi convention when a crossing guard at a local school motions for you to pull over. While you're embarrassed to hold up traffic, you are more embarrassed for the guard to see your costume. What are you wearing? What happens?

Postcard to Self. Write a note to yourself as if from a place you hope to visit someday.

You have just been approved to write for 20 minutes *without* a filter, internal editor, or the pressure of a panel of judges reading what you produce. Such freedom. What might happen if you let yourself feel this way every time you approach a blank page? (And honestly, how often *are* you writing for judges?) Enjoy!

What do you need today? Truly?

_____

_____

_____

_____

_____

_____

277

Describe an image that gives you peace.

_____

_____

_____

_____

_____

_____

_____

What were your favorite songs as a child? Tween? Young adult? Write down the titles and explore how it feels to recall them. Do they reflect a continuum or phases? Would you include them in the soundtrack of your life, or would you do some creative editing?

Make a list of seven of your most endearing characteristics and seven of your least lovable ones. Then draft a fictional character profile by borrowing a couple from each list.

_____   _____

_____   _____

_____   _____

_____   _____

_____   _____

_____   _____

"You are going to love some of your characters, because
they are you or some facet of you, and you are going to hate
some of your characters for the same reason."[22]

Anne Lamott

Writing Sprint. Choose a word to be your jumping-off point for a ten-minute writing session: *danger, country fair, tingling, lonely.*

"Thin place" is a term used to describe a setting or experience where the physical world and spiritual world are closest. Write about an experience you've had with a thin place or what it means to you to be close to the sacred.

Briefly research something or someone. Then quickly write an essay or blog post about one angle you discover.

283

When have you witnessed great courage and authenticity? Write about the experience.

 How might a current challenge be a gift?

Share your work more than you compare your work.

The word gets out that the eccentric founder of a small town buried a safe containing a million dollars somewhere in the community. Write as a tourist who comes upon the chaos.

Amy Cuddy is the social psychologist who struck a chord and pose with her TED Talk—and her book, *Presence*—about how our body positions influence our emotions and confidence.[23] Before you write today, pose like a superhero with hands on hips and a strong, wide stance—or keep that wide-legged position and raise your arms in a victory posture.

Today's writing topic: *The change I'd like to be in the world is...*

 **Body Prayer #9.** *Legs:* How have these limbs served you? Even if there has been pain or times they have faltered, consider what you can be thankful for: first steps, walking in nature, carrying you through stages of your life, pressing on in hard times, etc.

Write for 20 minutes on a pivotal life moment. What happened? What images, emotions, or sense triggers are strongest? What was the impact of that event on you? Describe who you were before that moment and who you've been since. Is there a change you might not have been aware of until now?

289

What do you do instead of writing? List the ways you avoid writing.

While attending a work convention, you go in search of the conference center restroom. On the way, you hear an '80s love song blaring from behind a slightly open door. Curious, you peek inside. A nervous woman wearing a "wedding planner" badge grabs your hand, ushers you to the front of a crowd, and announces it is time for the wedding toast. You are handed the mic.

Describe in detail the perfect job for you. Get creative. Hey, why not invent a job?

292

Write a heart response to this proverb from the Bible: "Speak up for those who cannot speak for themselves, for the rights of all who are destitute" (Proverbs 31:8).

Create a ritual around writing.

If you were one word, what word would that be? If your life were one sentence, what would that sentence be?

"A single word even may be a spark of inextinguishable thought."
Percy Bysshe Shelley

Write two haikus on world peace. (Remember, a haiku is a three-line poem with a five-seven-five syllable pattern.)

_____

_____

_____

_____

_____

_____

You did such a good job naming deodorants in #245, your agency has been flooded with requests for your genius. Invent two name options to pitch to clients for each of the needs listed below.

Extra challenge: Describe the unique products and their selling points.

Board game for kids ages 8 to 12:

Hamburger topped with squeaky cheese from Wisconsin:

Dance step for a trendy modern studio in town:

Taco sauce tinted purple:

Beach town sprouting up between two popular tourist spots:

Skydiving company housed at the Eiffel Tower in Paris:

Write an original proverb. Or three.

Examples of proverbs:

"Above all else, guard your heart,
for everything you do flows from it" (Proverbs 4:23).

"Good advice is often annoying;
bad advice never is" (French proverb).

💡 **Postcard to Self.** Write a note to your current self from your future self.

Dear Younger Me,

To: Me
101 The Past
Fordham;
Monad.

3701

Love,
Older Me

Create a roster of mentors, leaders, companions, or role models who have given you something positive. Next to each name, list the characteristic, strength, or encouragement you received. To close, write a paragraph about one of these examples.

💡 **Writing Sprint.** Choose a word to be your jumping-off point for a ten-minute writing session: *spiral, wingspan, solace, observer.*

300

You have been told to pack your bags, and you've been handed a plane ticket and an envelope. Where are you going, and what's in the envelope?

Only you think the way you do and write the way you do.

Choose a topic. For 20 minutes, write everything you know about it. Follow all threads that come to mind and keep writing to fill every bit of the page with insights, descriptions, and details. This practice will help you recognize how many of the things you know are linked. It's like playing "Six Degrees of Kevin Bacon" (look it up) for a useful purpose.

That was the last straw…

Write about a moment when you felt God was guiding you toward a decision, conversation, or direction.

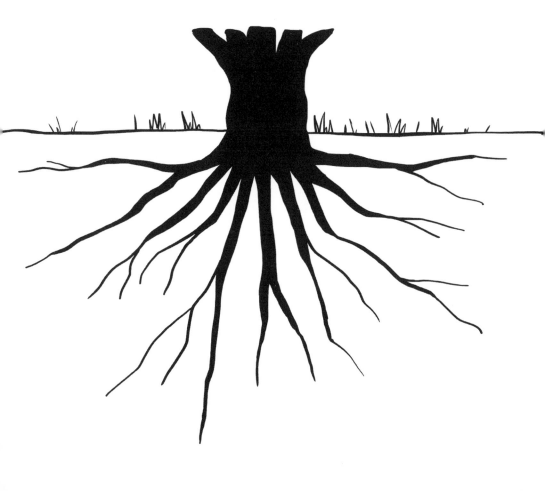

Your roots run deep. Which of your roots are people, experiences, beliefs? Some far-reaching roots have been a part of your foundation since birth. Others are newer, shorter sprouts which offer a different stability. Label each of the roots to better understand what holds you up and gives you life.

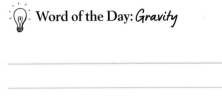

✎ Design a bookmark that somehow promotes you or your philosophy on the writing life.

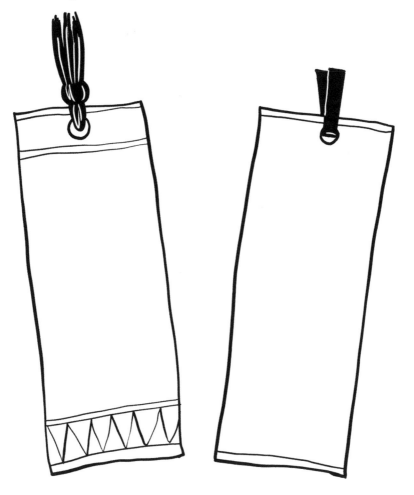

Ding-Dong. Special Delivery! You open the door. In your driveway are four modes of transportation and a sandwich board that reads: "Go explore." What are the four options, which do you choose, and where do you go?

Write about a moment in life, contrasting your thoughts at the time with your actions or voiced words.

Change chairs, rooms, or views to open the vistas of thought.

Describe your soul. Is it shiny, light, expansive, fluid? What does it hold? What does it do?

Create another blackout poem! This time from a piece by Mary Austin about the American Southwest. Blot out all the words that *aren't* your unique poem.

On the very edge of the black rock the earth falls away in a wide sweeping hollow, which is Shoshone Land. South the land rises in very blue hills, blue because thickly wooded with ceanothus and manzanita, the haunt of deer and the border of the Shoshones. Eastward the land goes very far by broken ranges, narrow valleys of pure desertness, and huge mesas uplifted to the skyline, east and east, and no man knows the end of it. It is the country of the bighorn, the wapiti, and the wolf, nesting place of buzzards, land of cloud-nourished trees and wild things that live without drink. Above all, it is the land of the creosote and the mesquite. The mesquite is God's best thought in all this desertness...Higher on the table-topped ranges low trees of juniper and piñon stand each apart, rounded and spreading heaps of greenness. Between them, but each to itself in smooth clear spaces, tufts of tall feathered grass. This is the sense of the desert hills, that there is room enough and time enough. Trees grow to consummate domes; every plant has its perfect work...Live long enough with an Indian, and he or the wild things will show you a use for everything that grows in these borders.[24]

Baggage. We all have it. Write words to describe or list your emotional and/ or physical baggage.

312

It's a Friday afternoon in a bustling city. You are standing among a crowd of strangers when a shocking event occurs. Describe the happening from your viewpoint. Then write about the incident from another character's perspective.

🖉 **A Book in You #10.** Write promotional copy for your book. Imagine this will appear on the back of the book, its marketing venues, or via online retail sites. Think through its benefits, appeal, value.

Make a list of names of/for God. Don't worry if they are names others use or not. Keep the list going. Tap into God's characteristics and nature.

315

Imagine that for the next month you'll only be able to *speak* the three sentences you choose to write down today. Do you write a personal message to yourself or someone you love? Do you choose a standard statement? Write the sentences below and why you chose them.

Pen a letter to a mentor or role model. Maybe someone you listed in prompt 298. Tell them what they specifically said or did and how it impacted your life. Consider sending this letter if that's a possibility.

317

Describe a time when you received a gift that made you feel special and known.

_____

_____

_____

_____

_____

_____

_____

_____

_____

_____

_____

_____

_____

_____

_____

_____

_____

_____

_____

Plan to attend a writers' conference or retreat.

318

Watch a TV or movie scene on mute. If you're away from technology (good for you!), position yourself so you can see but not hear people interacting. Now write a fictional account or script of what's happening. (It's like playing charades without telling the other people.)

319

Writing Sprint. Choose a word to be your jumping-off point for a ten-minute writing session: *invincible, door prize, retreat, cartwheel.*

320

List seven ways you are creative. Write more about the one you most enjoy. How does it feed your life?

Write about what happens internally when you make the effort to truly see a work of art. What thoughts emerge when you consider *yourself* to be a great piece of art crafted by the Creator?

"Great art is the result of hard work on the part of its creator, and therefore it sometimes demands a bit of work on the part of its audience—deeper and more focused attention than we are often used to giving in this fast-paced world of ours."[25]

Terry Glaspey

Write about a situation you want to hold lightly. Consider listing it on a separate piece of paper and putting the sheet into a fire or setting it aside for safekeeping so you don't feel obligated to overstress about it. Write about how it feels to loosen your grip.

323

A 35-year-old agoraphobic man in New Mexico, who hasn't left his home in a dozen years, receives notice that he is the sole heir to his wealthy uncle's estate. However, he must sign the papers in Chicago before he can receive the large sum. Write the scene when he makes his final decision to stay or go.

Imagine this page is a wall in a public square, and you are a graffiti artist. What design, phrase, or image will you create?

325

Describe your personal dream or "longed-for endeavor" in detail. Note how it will feel to pursue it and have kindred spirits show up as supporters, buyers, readers, etc. Who around you now might be a kindred spirit and source of encouragement as you move forward?

"You need only begin a pursuit of one dream or try out a longed-for endeavor and you will suddenly find kindred spirits all around."[26]

Joan Anderson

326

Craft another acrostic poem. This time use the word *compassion*. Let the word itself guide your thoughts as you start each poem line with the letters C-O-M-P-A-S-S-I-O-N. Don't judge the nudge to create. Go with it.

C _____

O _____

M _____

P _____

A _____

S _____

S _____

I _____

O _____

N _____

327

A Book in You #11. Write six interview questions you want members of the media to ask you during your book promotion season. (Write the answers too.)

328

💡 Word of the Day: *Resistance*

Name a goal that seems to be out of reach. Identify the main obstacle. Write a three-step plan of action to overcome the obstacle.

At your high school reunion, a former teacher tells you something that could've reshaped your sense of self or the course of your life, had he mentioned it to your teen self. What does he say? Why would it have made a difference?

💡 A funny thing happened on my way to…(Truth, tall tale, or whatever feels fun.)

_____

_____

_____

_____

_____

_____

_____

_____

_____

_____

_____

_____

_____

_____

_____

_____

_____

_____

_____

_____

_____

A blank page is a happy new beginning.

🌳 **Body Prayer #10.** *Hips:* What have you rested on your hips? Little ones, gro-ceries, firewood for a campout? With a written prayer, honor these moments and the ability to sit, stand, and move. Or appreciate aching hips that slow you down and invite you to rest.

333

Write a paragraph about a past happening in your life. See if an openness to the still, small voice allows you to notice what might want to be told. Read what you wrote and then write a new paragraph about the same happening to honor what wants to be heard.

"We have to believe that our story has as much to say as we do...Once we trust this, we are able to listen for what the story wants. So the challenge of revision is this: How can we get enough distance from the subject to see it in a new light? How can we step away from our agenda so we can hear the story's still, small voice?"[27]

Elizabeth J. Andrew

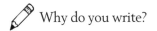 Why do you write?

 Write a blessing for yourself.

What was your first spoken word as a tot? Write about the significance of that word and if it has relevance to your life today.

_____

_____
_____
_____
_____
_____
_____
_____
_____
_____
_____
_____
_____
_____
_____
_____
_____
_____
_____
_____
_____

You are starting a worldwide movement. What is it, and why are you committed to this cause? Shape a mission statement.

Write about your relationship with technology. (You can be honest here on the page. No autocorrect will take over!)

339

✏️ Explain the inner workings of your mind. (Do you *dare*? Yes.)

Create a writing group or arrange regular writing dates.

**340**

💡 **Writing Sprint.** Choose a word to be your jumping-off point for a ten-minute writing session: *orphan, grasshopper, stain, lever.*

341

◉ Do a ten-minute writing session about your role in the universe. You have
one, you know.

_____

_____

_____

_____

_____

_____

_____

_____

_____

_____

_____

_____

_____

_____

_____

_____

_____

_____

_____

_____

 How is a flower like a prayer?

Write down the communication between two dogs who meet at a dog park while their owners strike up a conversation and make plans for a date.

✎ **A Book in You #12.** Congrats! You have finished the simplified steps to craft a book. Write about how it feels to have a plan. Even if you choose to write about something else, is there one aspect of this process that you can use as a launchpad?

_____

_____

_____

_____

_____

_____

_____

_____

_____

_____

_____

_____

_____

_____

_____

_____

_____

_____

_____

Spiritual Will #6. Now that you've done a few of the spiritual will writing prompts, consider piecing those together and expanding on them to craft a separate document for your spiritual will. Share with those you love the insights, matters of the heart, and prayers you have for them and the world. In this space, write more about your legacy of love and messages of encouragement and wisdom. It matters. Get it in writing.

346

Make a list of words you want to start using more often. Maybe you want more positive phrases in your speech and writing. Keep this list active and add to it even after you have finished this book.

347

Body Prayer #11. *Feet:* What makes your feet happy? Write a prayer or praise for the miles of life. Dancing. Leaping. Pushing off solid ground so your swing goes higher. Transporting you to a loved one.

Pretend you are your own therapist. Write out the dialogue that follows as you ask yourself questions about your childhood or your past year.

Think of a person whom you encounter occasionally. A barista, a bus driver, someone you pass on your weekly walk to the grocery store, etc. Now create a fictional backstory for this person as though they are a character in a novel.

350

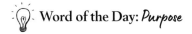

Word of the Day: *Purpose*

351

Go to a movie or think of one you've recently seen and write a review. Post the review online or share with the cinema lovers in your life.

352

Write the closing paragraph for a new book idea.

_____

_____

_____

_____

_____

_____

_____

_____

_____

_____

_____

_____

_____

_____

_____

_____

_____

_____

"I always write my last lines, my last paragraph, my last page first,
and then I go back and work towards it. I know where I'm going. I
know what my goal is. And how I get there is God's grace."[28]

Katherine Anne Porter

💡 **Writing Sprint.** Choose a word to be your jumping-off point for a ten-minute writing session: *fever dream, transformation, flip-flops, hide-and-seek.*

You are an established literary novelist who has been asked to ghostwrite a novel for a celebrity animated character. Yep. An invented character is getting an incredibly lucrative contract. If you accept the job, your fee would be substantial. Will you take it? Why or why not? Either way, write a scene for this novel at any point in the imagined storyline.

355

To look with compassion on a difficult time in your life, write about it in third person (she, he, hers, his) or second person (you, your).

Idea: Write in this space and then journal about how it feels to hold your experience in this new way.

Second-person example:

You had so much to juggle that year, and the expectations were high.

Third-person example:

He didn't realize so many things would change in such a short time.

Your search for meaning: Write about a topic you recently searched for online.

Prompts: Why did you search for it? What did you discover? Did the information lead to a next step, decision, regrettable purchase?

_____

_____

_____

_____

_____

_____

_____

_____

_____

_____

_____

_____

_____

_____

_____

_____

357

Hall pass! You're nearing the end of your unedited adventure, so write whatever your heart desires. Can you think of anything you haven't expressed or created that is aching to be transported to the page?

In her book *Invitation to Retreat*, Ruth Haley Barton shares, "The practice of retreat means we are fashioning a wilderness within that is always available and we can always return to."[29] Use this space to craft the schedule for a two-day retreat that would support writing, resting, spiritual renewal, and the "wilderness within." (And what does that phrase mean to you?)

In his early-twentieth-century book *Tremendous Trifles*, the clever G.K. Chesterton presents our fabulous prompt for the day: "Once I planned to write a book of poems entirely about the things in my pockets. But I found it would be too long; and the age of the great epics is past." Write a poem about what's in your pocket, backpack, purse, or laptop case.

360

Who introduced you to a love for or curiosity about words, reading, writing, dreaming, creating? Write about that person or those people and the point when you felt engaged. Was their encouragement given through words or actions?

Use chalk to share a happy message on your neighborhood sidewalk.

361

You know the classic grade-school essay, "What I did over vacation"? Write that...but make it up.

362

List ten reasons why you should keep up a daily writing practice. Have you convinced yourself?

1.

2.

3.

4.

5.

6.

7.

8.

9.

10.

End your day by writing.

 Before I go…

Postcard to Self. Write a note to yourself from the end of an experience or journey. Hey, how timely!

A **Book in You #13.** Use this page to practice signing your autograph. Be prepared to meet your public. Choose the right pen. Try a few writing styles.

Notes

1. Brenda Ueland, *If You Want to Write* (Minneapolis, MN: Graywolf, 1987), 14.

2. Eugene H. Peterson, *A Long Obedience in the Same Direction* (Downers Grove, IL: InterVarsity, 2000), 134.

3. Susan Zimmermann, *Writing to Heal the Soul* (New York, NY: Three Rivers, 2002), 140.

4. Langston Hughes, *The Collected Works of Langston Hughes*, ed. Arnold Rampersad, vol. 2, The Poems: 1941–1950 (Columbia, MO: University of Missouri Press, 2001), 65.

5. Susan G. Wooldridge, *Poemcrazy* (New York, NY: Three Rivers, 1996), 9-10.

6. Madeleine L'Engle, *Walking on Water* (Wheaton, IL: Harold Shaw, 1980), 81.

7. Zadie Smith, *Changing My Mind: Occasional Essays* (New York, NY: Penguin Books, 2009), 103.

8. M.F.K. Fisher, *The Gastronomical Me* (New York, NY: North Point, 1989), ix.

9. John O'Donohue, *Anam Cara* (New York, NY: HarperCollins, 1997), 71-72.

10. Thomas Merton, *Echoing Silence*, ed. Robert Inchausti (Boston, MA: New Seeds, 2007), 53.

11. Frederick Buechner, *Now and Then* (New York, NY: HarperOne, 1991), 87.

12. Jan L. Richardson, *In the Sanctuary of Women* (Nashville, TN: Upper Room, 2010), 262.

13. C.S. Lewis to Arthur Greeves, Great Bookham, 14 June 1916, *Letters of C.S. Lewis*, ed. W.H. Lewis and Walter Hooper (New York, NY: HarperOne, 2017), 56.

14. Christine Valters Paintner and Betsey Beckman, *Awakening the Creative Spirit* (New York, NY: Morehouse, 2010), 19.

15. Julia Cameron, *The Artist's Way* (New York, NY: Tarcher/Putnam, 1992), 18.

16. Gina Marie Mammano, *Camino Divina: Walking the Divine Way* (Woodstock, VT: SkyLight Paths, 2016), 23, 25-26.

17. Parker J. Palmer, *On the Brink of Everything* (Oakland, CA: Berrett-Koehler, 2018), 99.

18. Madeleine L'Engle, *The Irrational Season* (New York, NY: Seabury, 1979), 90.

19. Hope Lyda, *Life as a Prayer* (Eugene, OR: Harvest House, 2017), 65.

20. Pat Schneider, *Writing Alone and with Others* (New York, NY: Oxford University, 2003), 17.

21. Flannery O'Connor, *A Prayer Journal* (New York, NY: Farrar, Straus and Giroux, 2013), 11.

22. Anne Lamott, *Bird by Bird* (New York, NY: Anchor, 1995), 45.

23. Amy Cuddy, *Presence* (New York, NY: Back Bay, 2018).

24. Mary Austin, *The Land of Little Rain* (Boston, MA: Houghton, Mifflin and Company, 1904), https://archive.org/stream/landoflittlerain00aust/landoflittlerain00aust_djvu.txt.

25. Terry Glaspey, *75 Masterpieces Every Christian Should Know* (Grand Rapids, MI: Baker, 2015), 17.

26. Joan Anderson, *A Weekend to Change Your Life* (New York, NY: Broadway, 2006), 216.

27. Elizabeth J. Andrew, *Writing the Sacred Journey* (Boston, MA: Skinner House, 2005), 196.

28. Katherine Anne Porter, *Katherine Anne Porter: Conversations*, ed. Joan Givner (Jackson, MS: University Press of Mississippi, 1987), 88.

29. Ruth Haley Barton, *Invitation to Retreat* (Downers Grove, IL: InterVarsity, 2018), 125.

Connect with Hope Lyda at:

www.mywritedirection.com

Instagram
@mywritedirection

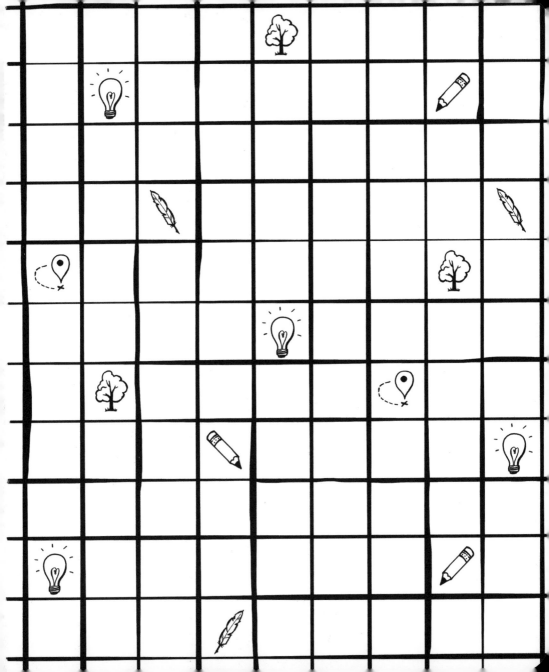

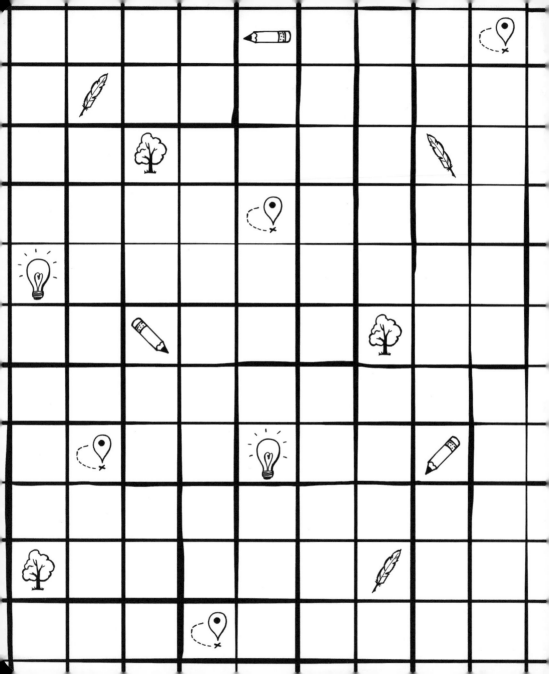